All-In-One Piano Lessons
Book A

FOREWORD

The **All-In-One Piano Lessons Books A and B** combine selected pages from the Piano Lessons, Technique, Solos, Theory Workbook, and Practice Games into one easy-to-manage book. Upon completion of the **All-In-One Piano Lessons Books A and B,** students will be ready to continue into the **All-In-One Piano Lessons Books C and D.** Upon completion of the **All-In-One Piano Lessons Books A, B, C, and D,** students are ready to progress to Level 3 of the **Hal Leonard Student Piano Library**.

When music excites our interest and imagination, we eagerly put our hearts into learning it. The music in the **Hal Leonard Student Piano Library** encourages practice, progress, confidence, and best of all – success! Over 1,000 students and teachers in a nationwide test market responded with enthusiasm to the:

- variety of styles and moods
- natural rhythmic flow, singable melodies and lyrics
- "best ever" teacher accompaniments
- improvisations integrated throughout the **Lesson Books**
- orchestrated accompaniments included in audio and MIDI formats.

When new concepts have an immediate application to the music, the effort it takes to learn these skills seems worth it. Test market teachers and students were especially excited about the:

- "realistic" pacing that challenges without overwhelming
- clear and concise presentation of concepts that allows room for a teacher's individual approach
- uncluttered page layout that keeps the focus on the music.

The **Hal Leonard Student Piano Library** is the result of the efforts of many individuals. We extend our gratitude to all the teachers, students and colleagues who shared their energy and creative input. May this method guide your learning as you bring this music to life.

Best wishes,

Barbara Kreader   Fred Kern   Phillip Keveren   Mona Rejino

Authors
Barbara Kreader, Fred Kern, Phillip Keveren, Mona Rejino

Manager, Educational Piano
Jennifer Linn

Editor
Anne Wester

Illustrator
Fred Bell

To access audio visit:
www.halleonard.com/mylibrary

Enter Code
2878-1496-8621-6884

ISBN 978-1-4234-6111-1

HAL•LEONARD® CORPORATION
7777 W. BLUEMOUND RD. P.O. BOX 13819 MILWAUKEE, WI 53213

Visit Hal Leonard Online at
www.halleonard.com

CONTENTS

WHITE-KEY GROUPS

C D E | F G A B

* Students can check pieces as they play them.

SITTING AT THE PIANO

Ask yourself:

Am I sitting tall but staying relaxed?

Are my wrists and elbows level with the keys of the piano?

HAND POSITION

1) Let your arms hang relaxed at your sides. Notice how your hands stay gently curved.

2) Keep your hands relaxed and curved as you raise them to the piano keyboard.

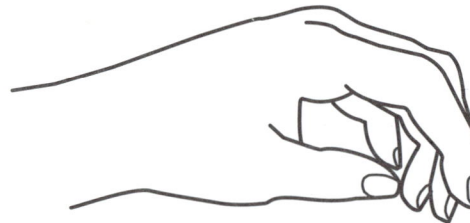

3) When you are playing the piano, keep your fingers in this relaxed, curved position.

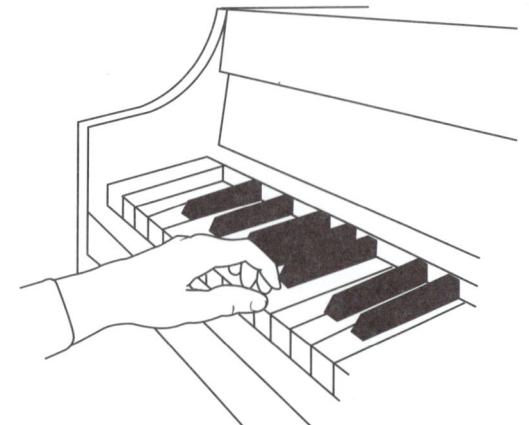

Feel The Beat!

Become aware of the heartbeat inside your body. Feel how it beats in an even pulse. Sometimes your heart beats fast, like when you run; sometimes it beats slowly, like when you are asleep, but it always beats evenly.

Rhythm In Music

Music has a pulse, too. Just like your heartbeat, musical pulse can go fast or slow.

Clap this pulse as your teacher plays the accompaniment below three different times at different speeds:

1) at a slow speed,   2) at a medium speed,   3) at a fast speed.

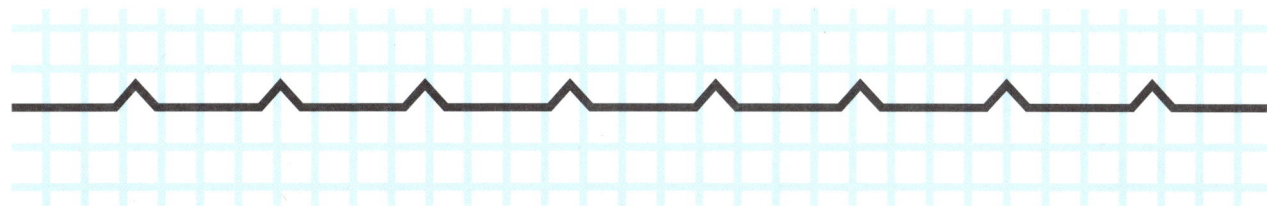

You can also play this pulse on the piano using any black key. Remember to keep the pulse even.

The orchestrated accompaniment track numbers indicate slow, medium, and fast speeds.

🔊 1/2/3

Accompaniment

Repeat as necessary | *Last time*

5

Feel the Beat!
(Activity Page)

Sit quietly and listen to your heartbeat.
Feel how it beats with a steady pulse.

1. Circle the things that have a steady beat.

2. Draw a picture of something that makes a steady, ticking sound.

FINGER NUMBERS

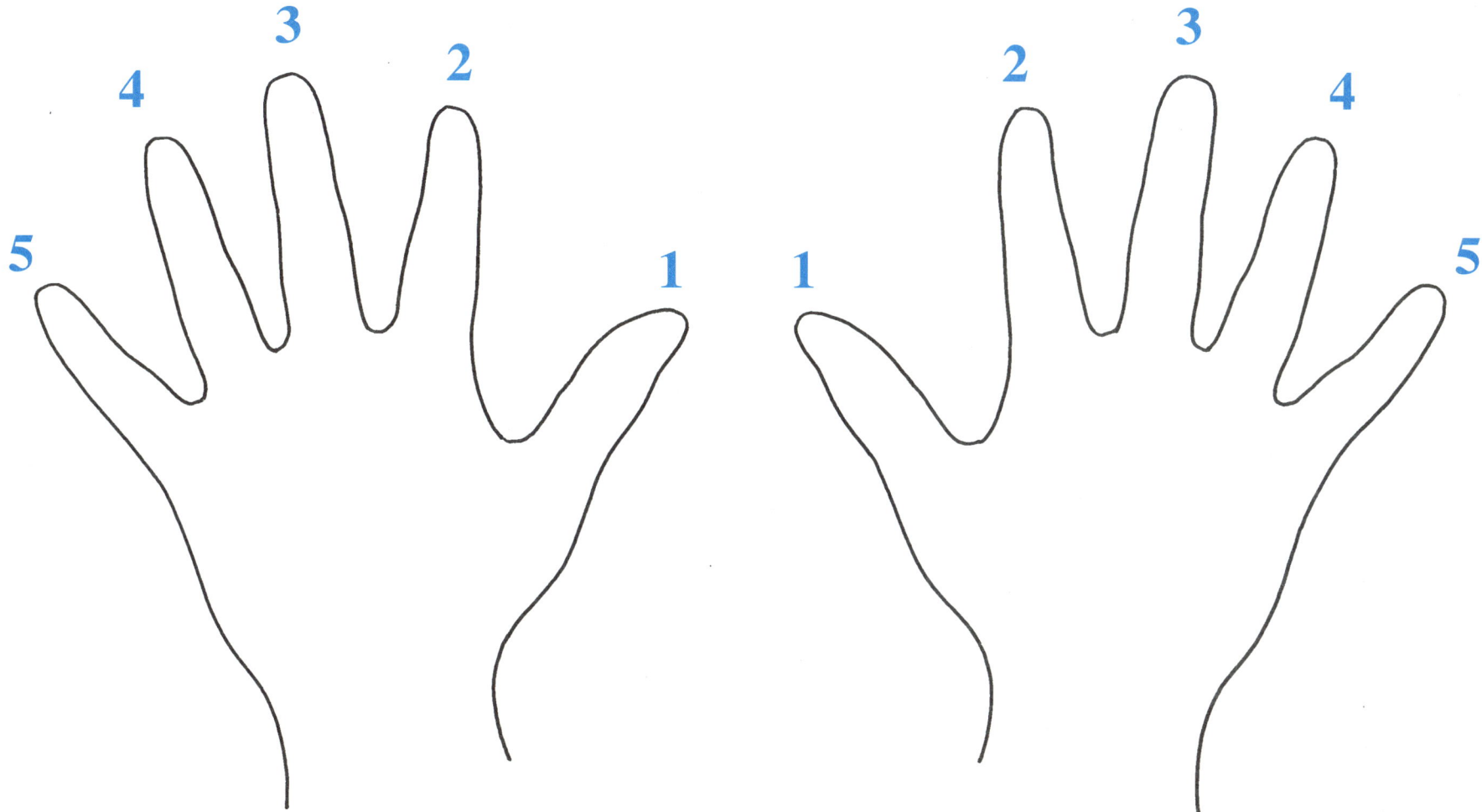

Place your hands together with fingertips touching.

Tap your 1st fingers (thumbs).
Tap your 2nd fingers.
Tap your 3rd fingers.
Tap your 4th fingers.
Tap your 5th fingers.

Tap 4s,   tap 2s,   tap 5s,   tap 1s,   tap 3s.

7

Number That Finger!

Which fingers are wearing the rings?
Write the correct finger number in each box.

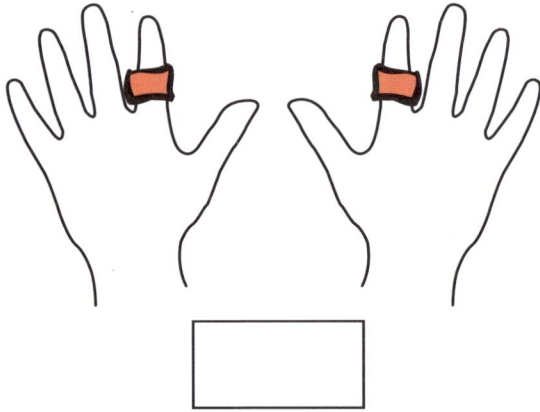

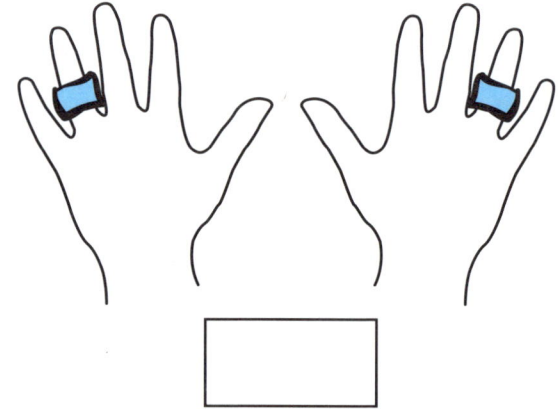

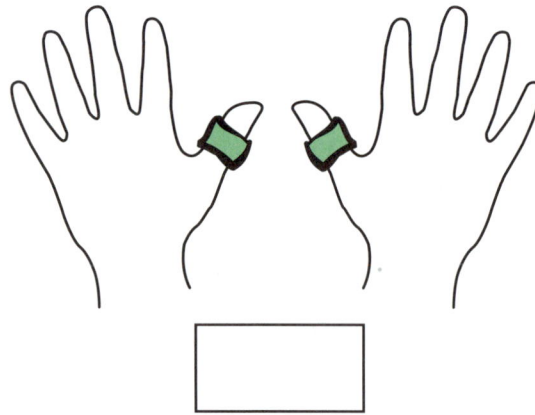

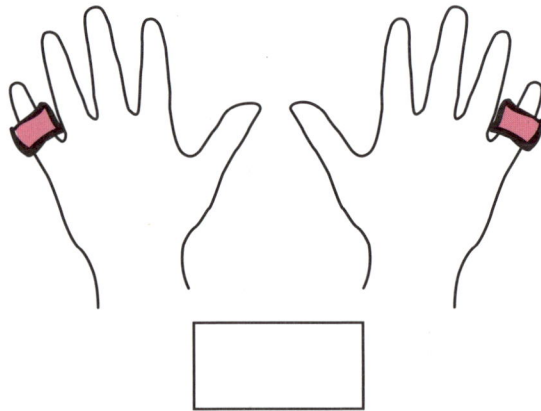

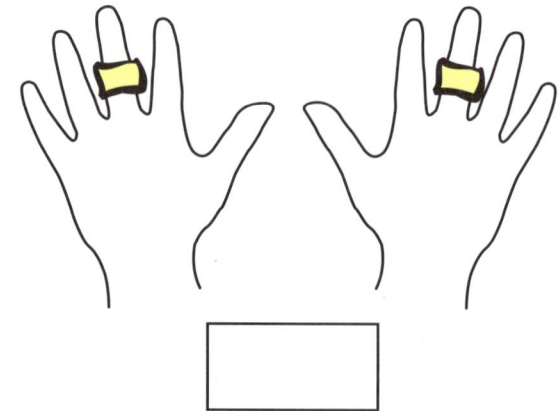

THE PIANO KEYBOARD

The piano keyboard is divided into sets
of two and three black keys.

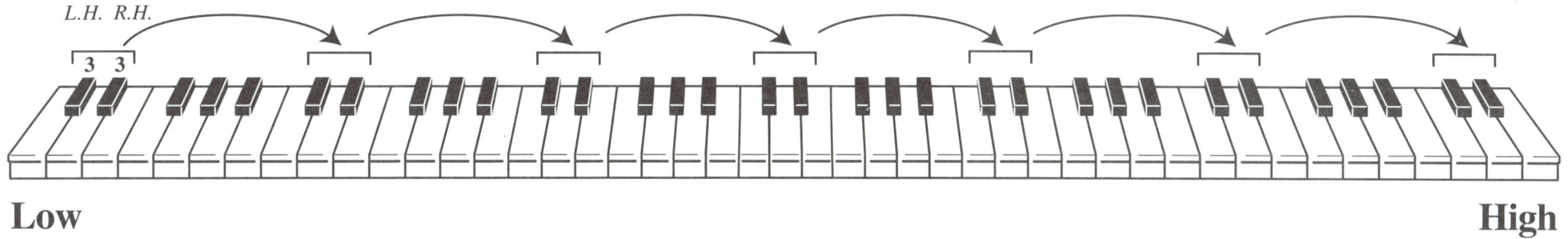

L.H. R.H.

Low

High

TWO BLACK KEYS

Put your thumbs behind the
first joint of your third fingers
and use your third fingers to
play the groups of two black
keys. Start at the low end of the
keyboard and play higher.

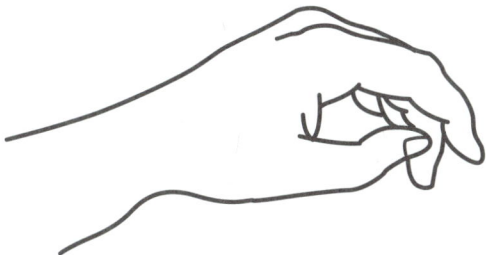

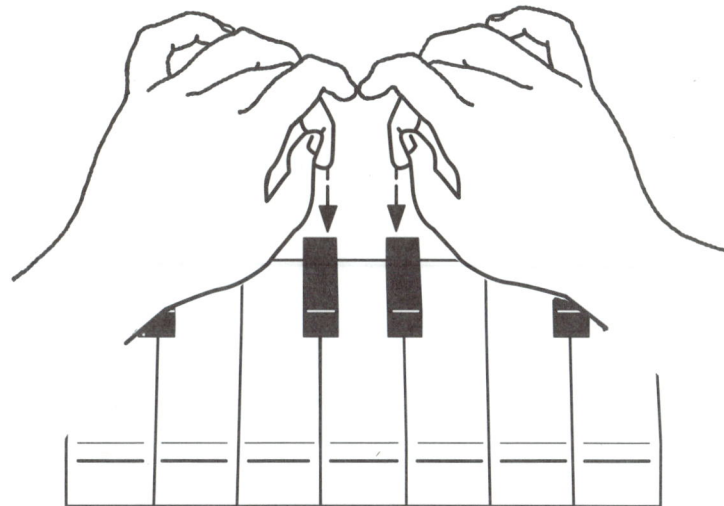

When you play the pieces
"Climbing Up" and "Climbing
Down" on pages 12 and 13,
you will play the groups of
two black keys as shown here.

9

Circle each set of two blackbirds.

Two Black Keys

Color each set of two black keys.

On the piano: Play two black keys way down low.
Play two black keys way up high.

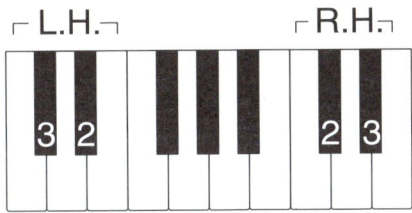

Grandfather's Clock

These small black boxes are called "clusters."
Play notes together using fingers indicated.

Keep "ticking" to the end.

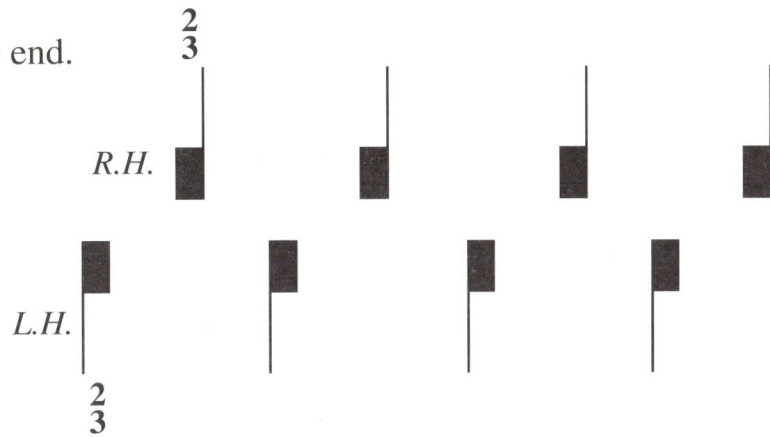

R.H.

L.H.

Play Again

Henry Clay Work

With accompaniment, student starts here:

4/5

Tick Tock (♩=100)

Grand - fa - ther's clock was too large for the shelf, so it stood nine - ty years on the floor.
Tal - ler by half than the old man him - self 'tho it weighed not a pen - ny weight more.

Climbing Up

Two Black Keys
Moving Up The Keyboard

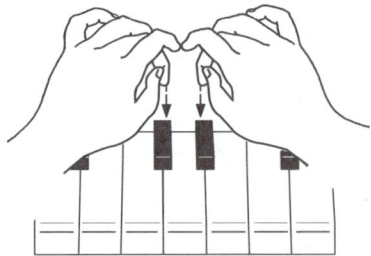

Play this song on two black keys with the third finger in each hand.

It is helpful to clap and sing the words of a piece before playing it. Remember to keep a steady pulse!

High - er, high - er look at me!

R.H.

L.H.

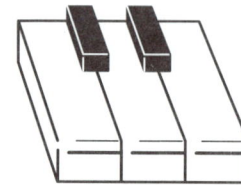

Climb - ing, climb - ing up this tree,

R.H.

L.H.

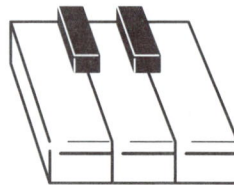

With accompaniment, student starts here:

🔊 **6/7**

With determination (♩ = 120)

mf

8va -

12

Climbing Down

Two Black Keys
Moving Down The Keyboard

Care - ful   as   I'm climb -ing down,

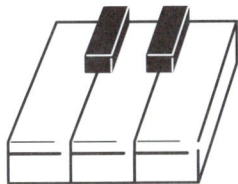

R.H.

L.H.

Low - er, low - er, touch the ground.

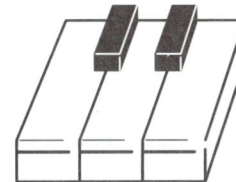

R.H.

L.H.

"Climbing Up" and "Climbing Down" can also be played as one song.

With accompaniment, student starts here:

With determination (♩ = 120)

mf

8va -

My Own Song

With your right and left hands, choose any groups of two black keys in the upper part of the piano.

Listen and feel the pulse as your teacher plays the accompaniment below. When you are ready, play along and make up your own song.

Have fun!

Accompaniment 🔊 8

Flowing
(♩ = 100)

Repeat as necessary

Last time

THREE BLACK KEYS

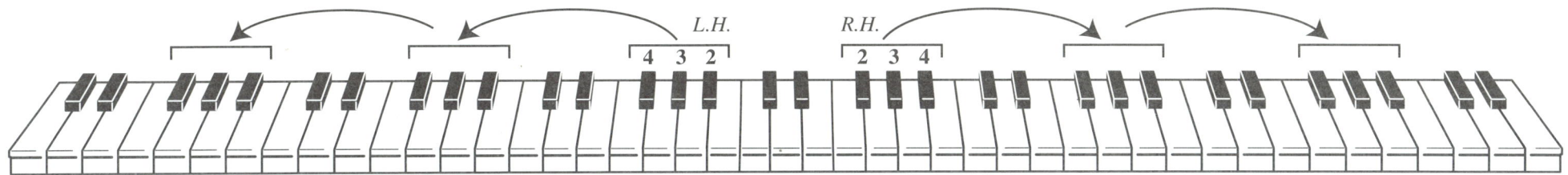

L.H. 4 3 2   R.H. 2 3 4

Low

High

Using your **left hand**, start in the middle of the keyboard and play the groups of three black keys with fingers 2-3-4 going **down the keyboard**.

Using your **right hand**, start in the middle of the keyboard and play the groups of three black keys with fingers 2-3-4 going **up the keyboard**.

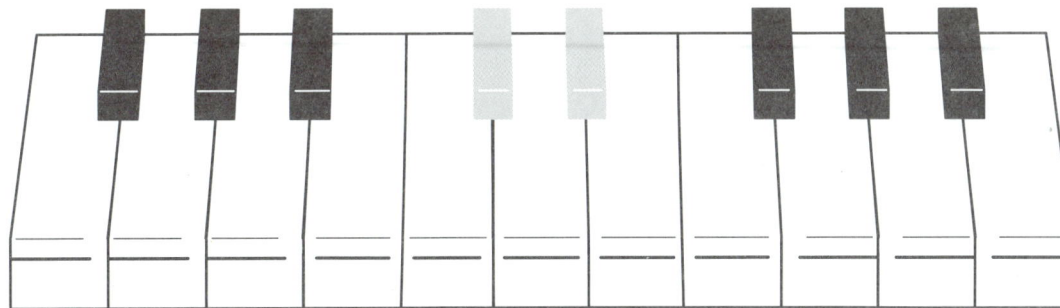

Play "My Own Song" again, using the groups of three black keys.

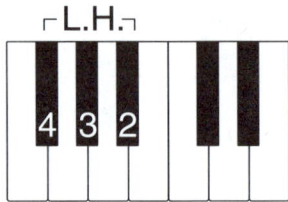

When you play these pieces by yourself, use the middle of the keyboard.

It is helpful to clap the rhythm of a piece before playing it.

QUARTER NOTE

Notes tell us how long the sounds last.
A **Quarter Note** lasts for one pulse (beat).

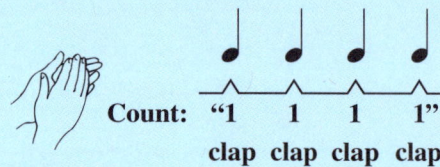

Count: "1   1   1   1"
clap clap clap clap

QUARTER REST

Rests are pictures of silence.
A **Quarter Rest** lasts for one pulse (beat).

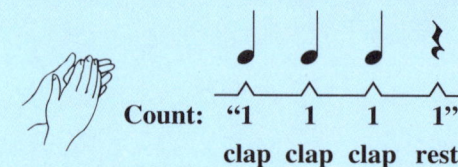

Count: "1   1   1   1"
clap clap clap rest

My Dog, Spike

Steady

"Hot Cross Buns"

My   dog,   Spike,   off   to   school,   out   to   prove   that   he's   so   cool.

L.H.   2   3   4   2   3   4   4   4   3   3   2   3   4

With accompaniment, student starts here: 9/10

Steady (♩ = 120)

mf

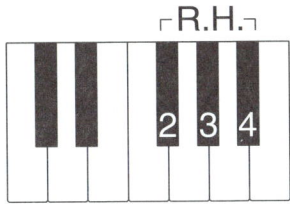

You can play "My Dog, Spike"
and "Sorry, Spike" as one song.

Sorry, Spike

Steady

R.H.

"Sor - ry, Spike!   You won't pass!   Bark - ing is - n't taught in class!"

With accompaniment, student starts here:

Steady (♩ = 120)

mf

Party Cat's Bubbles

Party Cat loves to make bubbles.
Trace and color each one.

Notes

Notes are pictures of sound.

Turn Party Cat's bubbles into notes.
Trace and color each one.

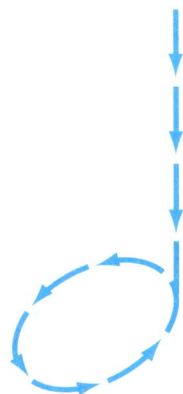

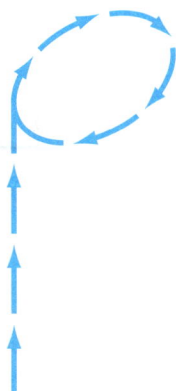

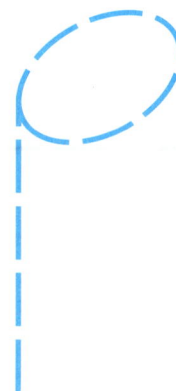

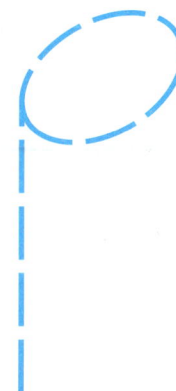

My Dog, Spike
(Activity Page)

1. As you listen to *My Dog, Spike*, clap and count the following rhythm two times:

2. Trace and color the quarter notes: Trace the quarter rests:

3. Complete the rhythm for *My Dog, Spike* by drawing the pictures of sound (♩) and the pictures of silence (𝄽) in the boxes below. When you are finished, tap and count the rhythm you wrote.

My	dog,	Spike,		off	to	school,		out	to	prove	that	he's	so	cool.
♩	♩	♩	𝄽				𝄽							♩ 𝄽

Left Hand

Left or Right?
Write "L.H." in the left hands and "R.H." in the right hands.

Right Hand

4 3 2   2 3 4

WHOLE NOTE

𝅝

A **Whole Note** fills the time of four quarter notes.

= 4 beats

𝅝 = 4 beats

Count: "1   2   3   4"

clap - hold - hold - hold

Merrily We're Off To School

Bouncy

"Mary Had A Little Lamb"

R.H.

4   3   2   3   4   4   4   3   3   3   4   4   4

Mer - ri - ly   we're   off   to   school,   off   to   school,   off   to   school.

With accompaniment, student starts here:

🔊 **11/12**

Bouncy (♩ = 130)

mf

22

These small black boxes are called "clusters."
Play notes together using fingers indicated.

Here's   our   school   bus.   Honk! Honk! Honk!   Hur - ry,   it   won't   wait.

L.H.
2   3   4   3   2   2   2   3   3   2   3   4
                                         3   3   3
                                         4   4   4

8va - - ⌐

23

Merrily We're Off To School
(Activity Page)

🔊 11

**Technique Tunes
by Katherine Glaser**

As you listen to *Merrily We're Off To School*, play this **Technique Tune**. Use energy from your whole arm, keeping your fingers close to the keys.

⌐ L.H. ⌐   ⌐ R.H. ⌐

4 3 2   2 3 4

Repeat as necessary.

4
3
2

R.H.

Honk! Honk! Honk!   Honk! Honk! Honk!

Honk! Honk! Honk!   Honk! Honk! Honk!

L.H.

2
3
4

2
3
4

Long Shadows

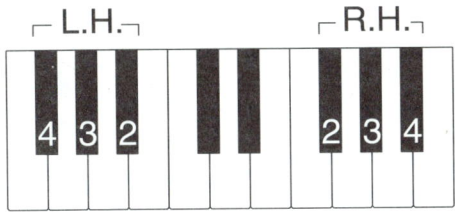

Slowly

R.H.

L.H.

With accompaniment, student starts here:

13/14

Slowly (♩ =80)

mp

1.

2.

HALF NOTE

A **Half Note** fills the time of two quarter notes.

= 2 beats

= 2 beats

Count: "1 2"
clap-hold

My Best Friend

"Pierrot"

Happily

R.H.

My best friend is *Ad - am.
              Mag - gie.

We play ev - 'ry day.

Hey, we just got start - ed, I wish s/he could stay.

L.H.

Play the first line of the song with your right hand; then play the second line of the song with your left hand.
*Fill in the name of your own friend.

With accompaniment, student starts here: 15/16

Happily
(♩ = 120)

"So long!"

mf

26

I Can Do It!

Barbara Kreader

L.H. 4 3 2   **R.H.** 2 3 4

MEASURES

Bar Lines group beats into **Measures**.

bar lines

measure   measure

With confidence

R.H.

4 3 2

I play key - board all day long.

4 3 2

Uh - oh, wrong notes.

L.H. 2 3 4

I go on.

2 3 4

R.H. 4 3 2

I can do it, here's my song.

Double Bar Line means the end of the piece.

Now it's right with no notes wrong!

L.H. 4 3 2 3 4

With accompaniment, student starts here:

🔊 **17/18**

With confidence (♩ = 120)

mf

27

I Can Do It!
(Activity Page)

Repeated Notes
Trace two repeated notes:

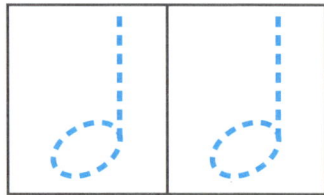

Stepping Down
Trace two notes stepping down:

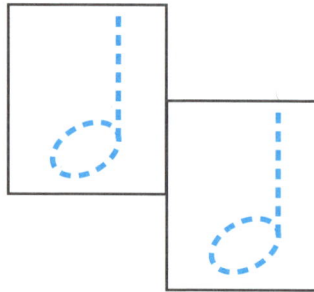

Stepping Up
Trace two notes stepping up:

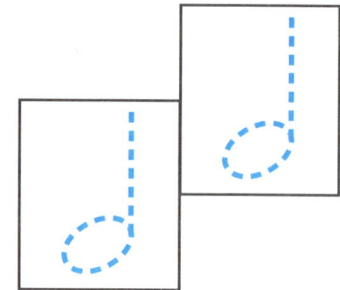

Complete this picture of *I Can Do It!*

1. Draw notes in the boxes and finger numbers in the blanks.
2. Play what you have written.

R.H. 4

L.H. 4

Which Hand Plays?

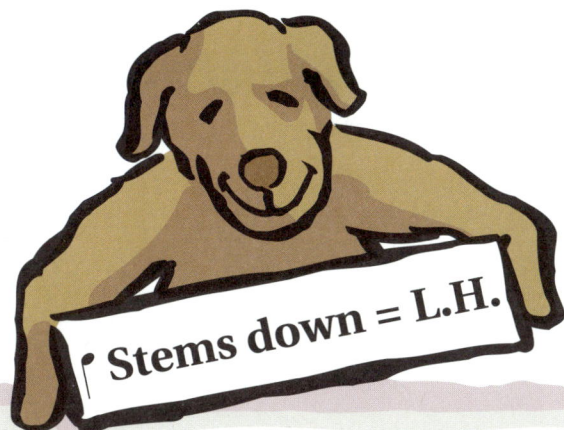

Stems down = L.H.

Circle the hand that plays each note.

Stems up = R.H.

L.H. R.H.   L.H. R.H.   L.H. R.H.

Draw the stem to match each hand.

L.H.   **R.H.**

L.H.   **R.H.**   **L.H.**

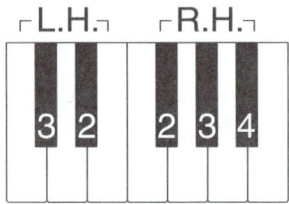

Let's Get Silly!

With excitement

Barbara Kreader

HALF REST

A **Half Rest** fills the time of two quarter rests.

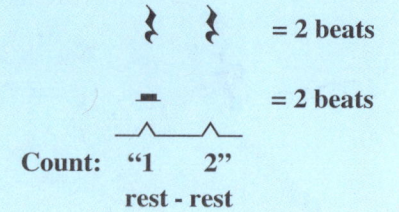

= 2 beats

= 2 beats

Count: "1   2"
rest - rest

R.H. 4
Come   play   in   the | 3 yard   with   me; | 2 laugh   and   twirl   a - | round.   **L.H.** 3

L.H. Tick - le   all   our | fun - ny   bones; | **R.H.** 4 fall   down   on   the | 3 ground.

With accompaniment, student starts here: 19/20

With excitement
(♩ = 130)

30

8va

R.H. **4** Make up jokes and | **3** cra - zy names; | **2** sing a fun - ny | song.

L.H. **3**

Laugh so hard that | we can't breathe. | **3** *R.H.* Bring a friend a - | **2** long.

L.H. **2** | **3**

Drawing Rests

shhh

A rest is a picture of silence.

Trace these quarter rests.

Trace these half rests.

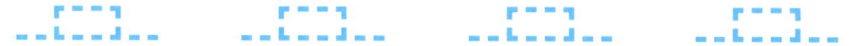

Your teacher will tap or play one of the rhythms in each box.
1. Circle the rhythm you hear.
2. Choose one note on the piano and play the rhythm you circled.

1.

2.

3.

Rhythm Detective

Find the missing notes and rests!

A note or rest is missing from every measure below. When completed, every measure has exactly four beats.

1. Choose a correct note or rest from the detective's hat.
2. Draw the missing note or rest in the box in each measure.

1.

2.

3.

4.

5.

Now it's your teacher's turn to guess!
Choose a note on the piano and play one of the five rhythms keeping a steady pulse.
Ask your teacher to guess which rhythm you played.

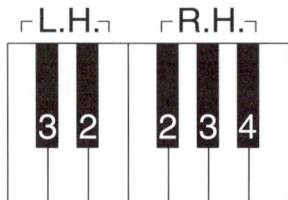

Water Lily

Phillip Keveren

Delicately

R.H.

2   3   4   4   2   3   4

Float - ing   in   the   wa   -   ter,   frag - ile   and   se   -   rene.

L.H.

3   2   3   2

R.H.

4   3   2   4   3   2   2

Such   a   splash   of   col   -   or   in   a   sea   of   green.

L.H.

2   3   3   2

With accompaniment, student starts here: 🔊 21/22

Delicately (♩=95)

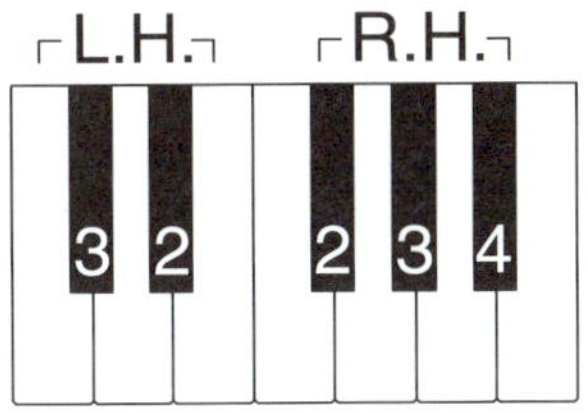

Mister Machine

Bill Boyd

Deliberately

R.H.

Squeak, whir, click, purr, boom, thunk, thunk. Nuts and bolts and bits of junk.

L.H.

Squeak, whir, click, purr, boom, clang, clang. What a ro - bot! Oops! Bang! Bang!

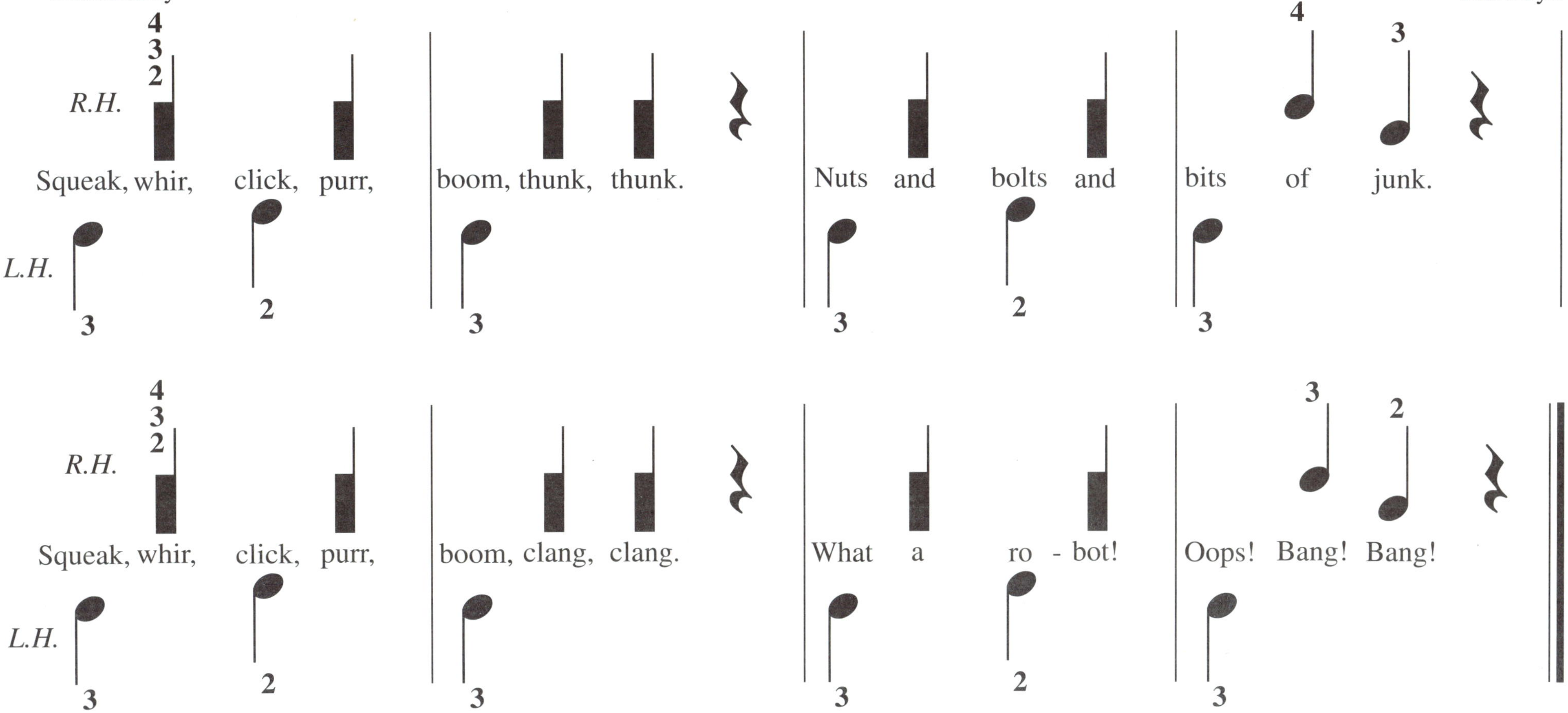

With accompaniment, student starts here:

23/24

Deliberately (♩ = 130)

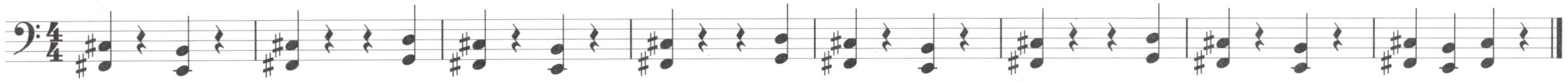

35

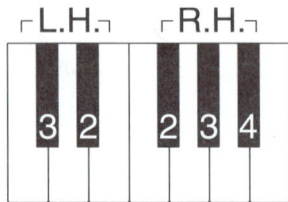

Walking The Dog

L.H. R.H.
3 2 2 3 4

Lazy   Fred Kern

R.H.

Walk,   scam - per   up - hill, down - hill.   Stop,   look, then   move a - long.

L.H.

R.H.

Bark,   sniff, and   growl   at   noth - ing.   Turn   and   head   back   home.

L.H.

With accompaniment, student starts here: 🔊 25/26

Lazy (♪♪ = ♪ ♪) (♩ = 105)

mp

36

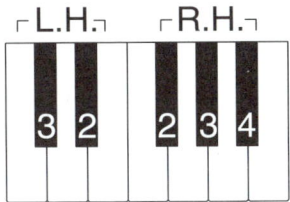

Night Shadows

Barbara Kreader

Quietly

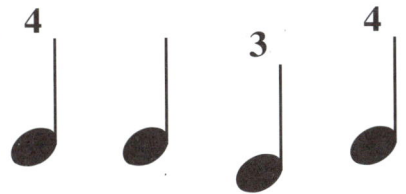 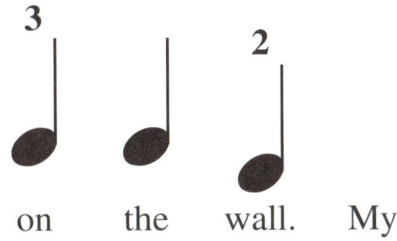 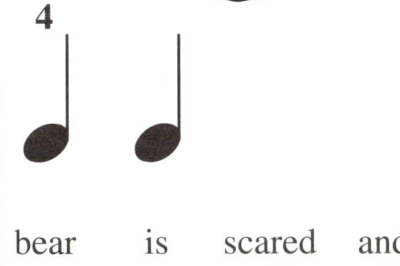 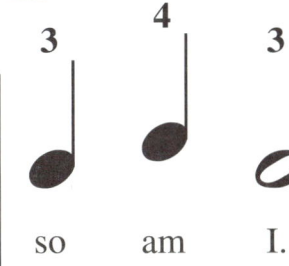

Shad - ows, shad - ows | on the wall. My | bear is scared and | so am I.

  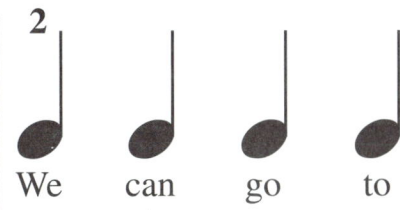

But my night light's | shin - ing. | We can go to sleep.

With accompaniment, student starts here: 🔊 27/28

Quietly (♩ = 82)

p

With pedal

37

Night Shadows
(Activity Page)

27

As you listen to *Night Shadows*, tap and count the following rhythm. Remember, ♩ = R.H. ♩ = L.H.

38

Rhythm Composer

Each fish bowl contains the notes and rests
you will need to compose the measures below.

1-beat fish bowl

4-beat fish bowl

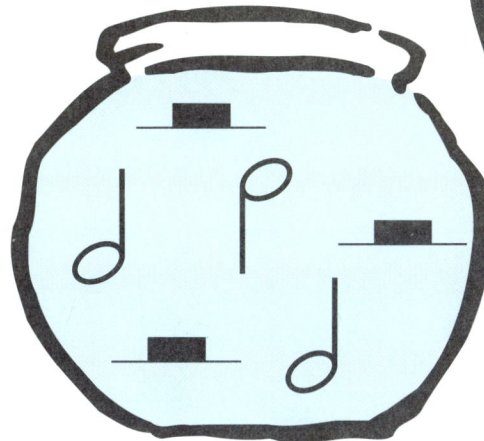

2-beat fish bowl

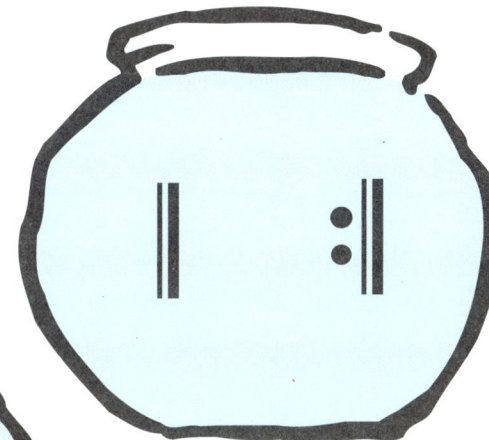

double bar
repeat sign
(means to play
the piece again)

Each measure needs exactly four beats.
Choose notes or rests from each fish bowl and draw them in the measures below.

bar line

bar line

Add a double bar

bar line

Add a repeat sign

THE MUSICAL ALPHABET

Playing on the White Keys

Music uses the first seven letters of the alphabet. These letters are used over and over to name the white keys.

With your right-hand third finger, play and sing the music alphabet three times, using this rhythm:

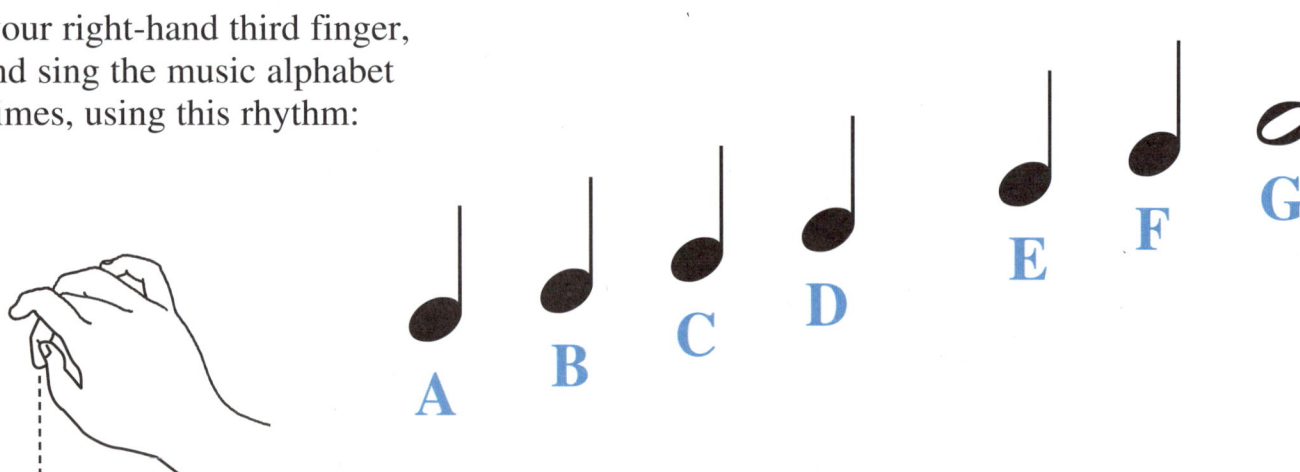

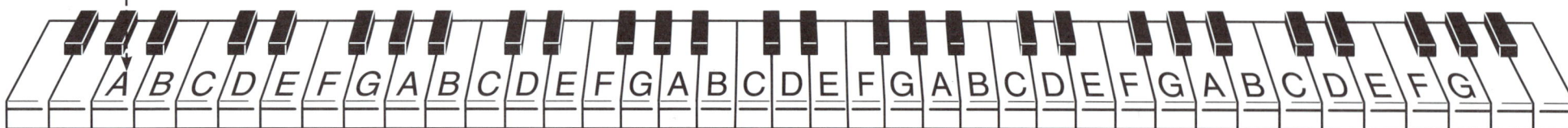

Alphabet Soup

Student part to be played by rote. 🔊 29

Fred Kern

Steady (♩ = 120)

40

The Musical Alphabet

B C D E F G

A

A B C D E F G

On each keyboard below, start with the given letter and write the musical alphabet.
The arrows will direct you to write the alphabet forwards or backwards.

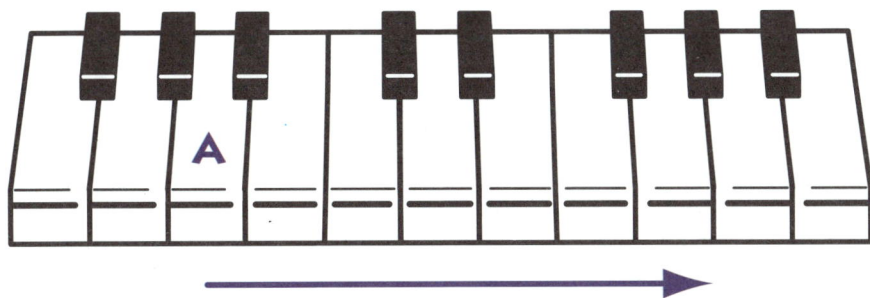

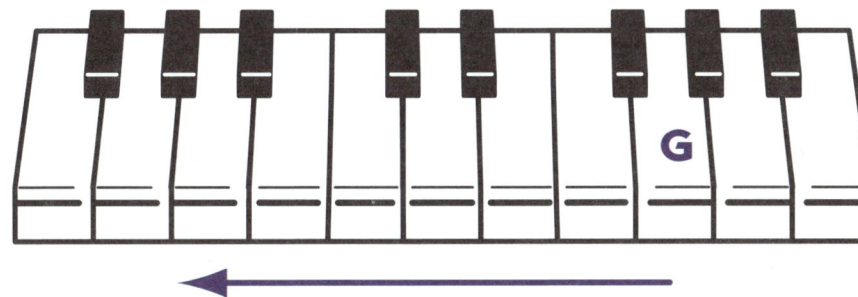

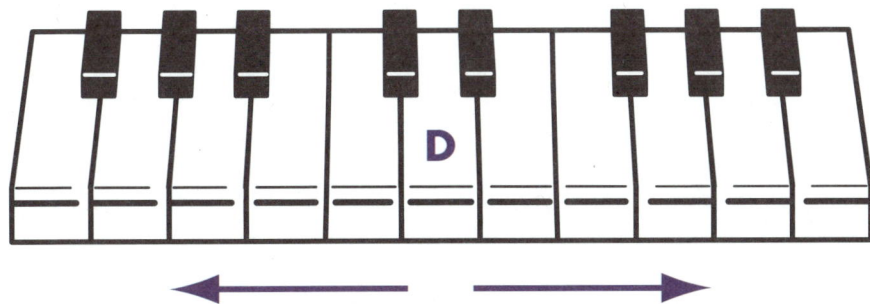

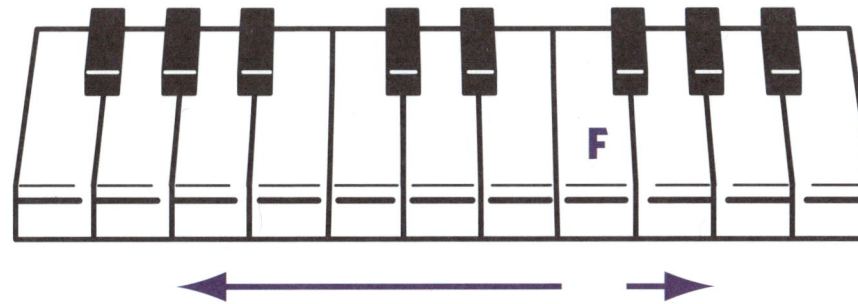

A

G

D

F

41

The Attic Stairs

Sing the musical alphabet forward and backward as you play "The Attic Stairs." Keep your thumb behind the first joint of your third finger.

Climb the stairs **two** times. Use finger 3.
  1. R.H. alone.
  2. L.H. alone.

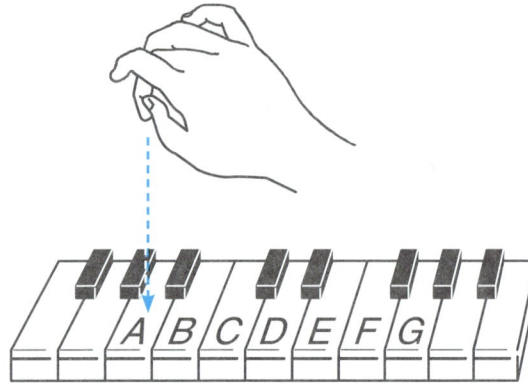

A B C D E F G

Repeat Sign means to play the piece again.

With accompaniment, student starts here: 🔊 **30/31**

Slowly (♩=100)

mp

42

C D E GROUPS

R.H.

C D E   C D E   C D E   C D E   C D E

1 2 3

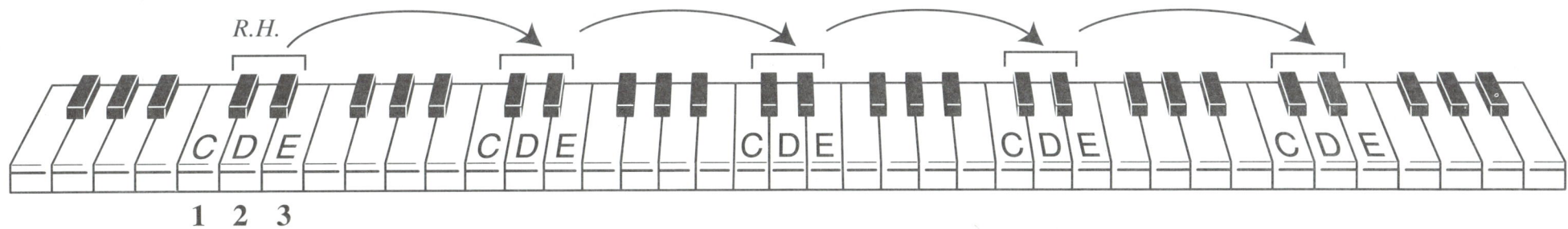

With your right hand, start at the low end of the keyboard and play
the C D E groups with individual fingers 1-2-3 going up the keyboard.

C D E

Now explore the keyboard,
playing the C D E groups
with your left hand using
fingers 3-2-1.

C D E Groups
(Activity Page)

1. Circle the sets of two black keys.
2. Write the C D E letter names on the white keys.
3. Color the C's red, the D's blue, and the E's green.

My Own Song
On C D E

With your right or left hand, choose any C D E group in the upper part of the piano.

Listen and feel the pulse as your teacher plays the accompaniment below. When you are ready, play C D E. Experiment by playing E D C.

Mix the letters any way you want and make up your own song.

Have fun!

Accompaniment 🔊 **32**

Flowing (♩ = 85)

Repeat as necessary

With pedal

45

Finding C D E
on the Keyboard

Party Cat is inviting some animal friends to his birthday party,
but he can't remember how to spell all their names.

Help him by filling in the missing letters.
1. Write the name of each outlined key in the blank below it.
2. Color the C's red, the D's blue, and the E's green.

____og   snak____   ____at   ____ow

____olphin   ____anary   monk____y

bir____   tig____r   ____onkey   ____row

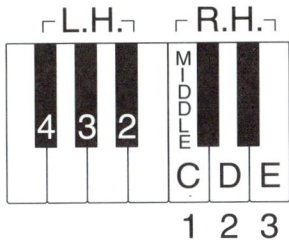

Balloon Ride

Phillip Keveren

Soaring

p What a day for fly - ing, sun is in my eyes.
Reach - ing for the heav - ens, float - ing through the skies.

Hold down the right pedal (damper pedal) throughout.

With accompaniment, student starts here:

33/34

Soaring (♩ = 120)

L.H. ***p***

47

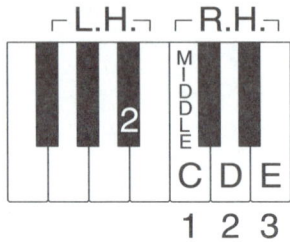

Party Cat

Phillip Keveren

Rockin'

R.H.

3 **2** **1** **1** **1**

Rock 'n' roll is | where it's at | for my fam - 'ly's | par - ty cat.

f

L.H. **2** **2** **2**

R.H.

3 **2** **1** **1** **1**

Lies a - round and | sleeps all day, | rocks the night a - way!

L.H. **2** **2**

With accompaniment, student starts here: 🔊 **35/36**

Rockin'

($\quad$ = 110)

mf

Bad cat!

48

Imagine & Create

Write in the C D E groups on the keyboard below.

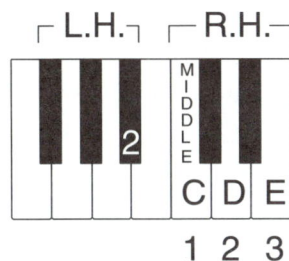

C

Improvise your own piece.

1. Choose one of the C D E groups on your piano and place your hands in the *Party Cat* position. Make your own piece using the keys pictured here:

2. Play along as you listen to the accompaniment to *Party Cat*. 🔊 **36**

3. Make up more pieces as you play along with the accompaniment for *Balloon Ride*. 🔊 **34** Just remember to stay in the *Party Cat* position.

L.H.   R.H.

MIDDLE

2   C D E

1 2 3

Make a Party Game!

The Party Cat (bad cat!) mixed up the keys on the next page so you can't play his song.
See if you can put them back in order.

1. Cut out the cards and write the name of each key in the box on the back.

2. Arrange the cards on the music rack of your piano in the order that matches the words:

    "Rock 'n' roll is where it's at"

3. Practice naming the keys on your C D E flash cards.
    How fast can you name them without a mistake?

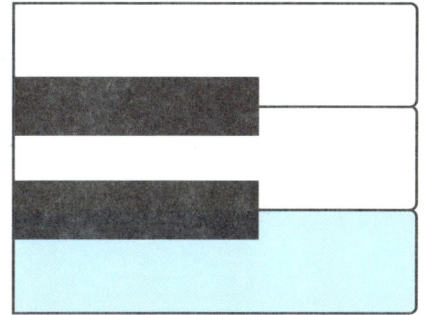
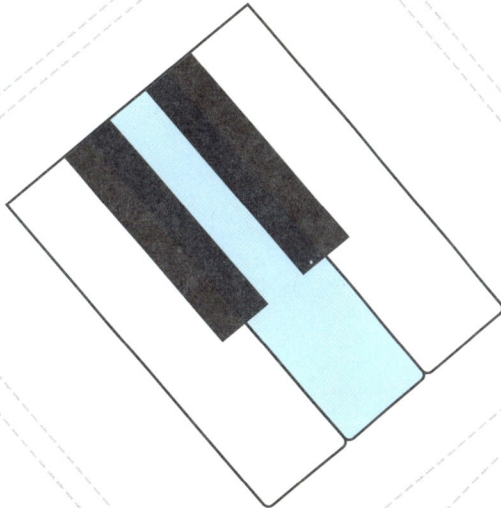
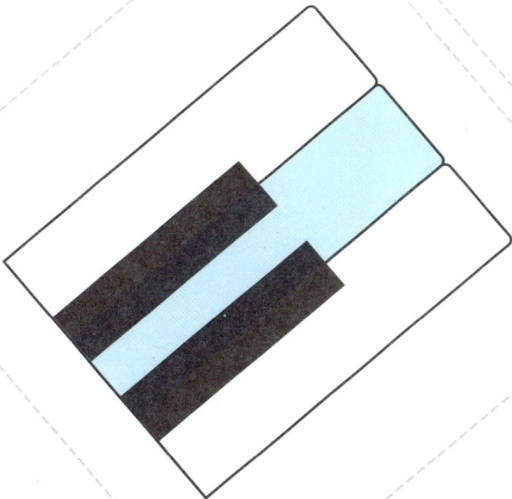

51

F G A B GROUPS

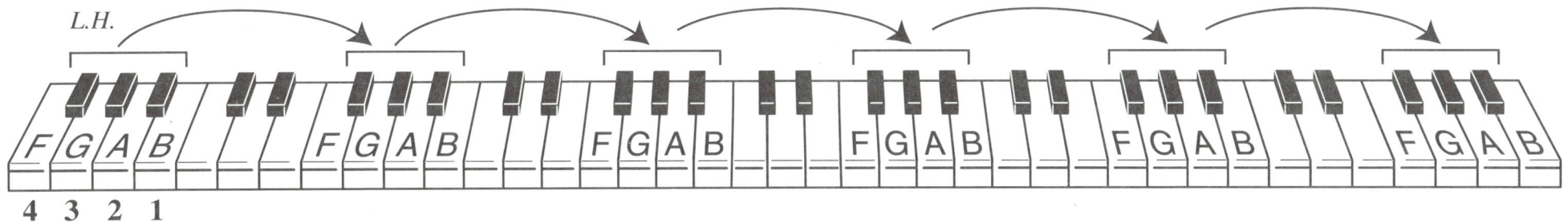

L.H.

4 3 2 1

With your left hand, start at the low end of the keyboard and play the
F G A B groups with individual fingers 4-3-2-1 going up the keyboard.

F G A B

Now explore the keyboard,
playing the F G A B groups
with your right hand using
fingers 1-2-3-4.

F G A B Groups
(Activity Page)

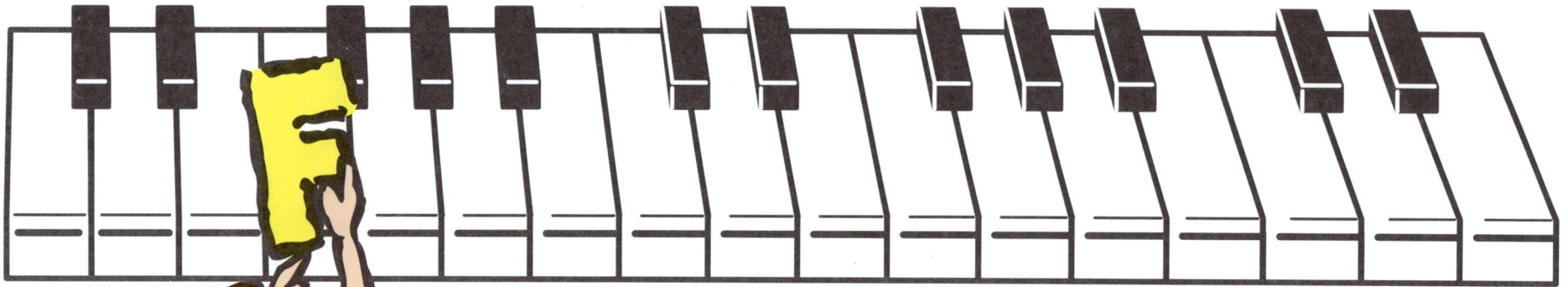

1. Circle the sets of three black keys.
2. Write the F G A B letter names on the white keys.
3. Color the F's yellow, the G's purple, the A's orange, and the B's brown.

My Own Song
On F G A B

With your left or right hand, choose any F G A B group in the upper part of the piano.

Listen and feel the pulse as your teacher plays the accompaniment below. When you are ready, play F G A B. Experiment by playing B A G F.

Mix the letters any way you want and make up your own song.

Have fun!

Accompaniment 🔊 **37**

Rock beat (♩ = 130)

Repeat as necessary | *Last time*

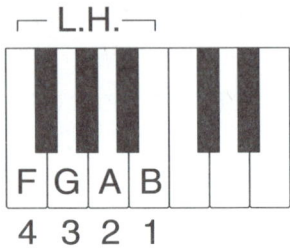

Monster Under My Bed

Phillip Keveren

Scary

L.H. **4**
p

3

4
f

3

2

1

2

3

4

With accompaniment, student starts here: 🔊 **38/39**

Scary (♩=86)

pp *poco a poco cresc.*

mf

Finding F G A B on the Keyboard

Spike is taking a taxi to his house at the end of Keyboard Lane.
Help the taxi driver follow Spike's directions to his house.

1. Circle the sets of three black keys.

2. Drive to the first F and color it yellow.

3. Drive to the next F and color it yellow.

4. Drive to the next A and color it orange.

5. Drive to the next G and color it purple.

6. Drive to the next B and color it brown.

7. Drive to the next G and color it purple.

8. Drive to the next A and color it orange.

9. Drive to the next F and color it yellow.

10. Drive to the next B and color it brown.

Hooray! Spike's home!

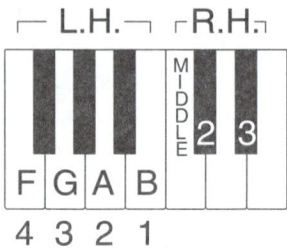

Taxi Tangle

Phillip Keveren

Impatiently

f

L.H.

Tax - i tan - gle | **on the high - way!** | R.H. **Honk! Honk!** | **Honk! Honk!**

Skid, bump! 'Xcuse me! | **Turned the wrong way!** | R.H. **Honk! Honk!** | **Honk!**

With accompaniment, student starts here: 40/41

Impatiently (♩ = 140)

mf

58

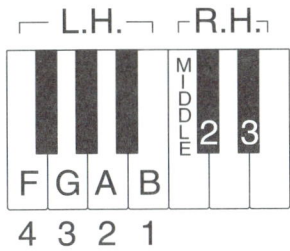

Undersea Voyage

Mysteriously

Phillip Keveren

R.H. **3**   **2**   **3**   **2**

p Deep   in - to   the   o - cean   in   my   sub - ma - rine.
  That's   the   big - gest   tur - tle   I   have   ev - er   seen!

L.H.   **1**   **2**   **3**   **4**   **1**   **2**   **3**

Hold down the damper pedal throughout.

With accompaniment, student starts here: 🔊 **42/43**

Mysteriously ($\quad$ = 120)

R.H.

$\frac{4}{4}$ *pp*   *L.H.*   **1.**   **2.**

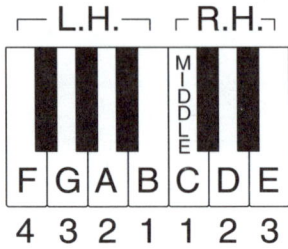

L.H. R.H.

F G A B C D E
4 3 2 1 1 2 3

TIME SIGNATURE

4/4 (4/4) = four beats fill every measure
= quarter note gets one beat

Count: "1　1　1　1 | 1　1　1 - 2 | 1 - 2 - 3 - 4"
or "1　2　3　4 | 1　2　3 - 4 | 1 - 2 - 3 - 4"

Sea (C) Song

Lively

Fred Kern

R.H.
1
C D E   C D E

f

L.H.
4
F G A B   F G A B

R.H.
1
C D E   C D E

L.H.
4
F G A B   F G A B

R.H.
1
C

With accompaniment, student starts here: 🔊 **44/45**

Lively
(♩ = 120)

mf

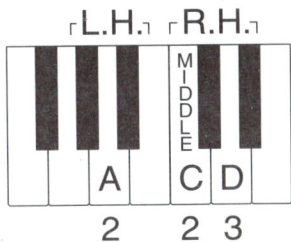

Rain, Rain, Go Away

Steady

Folk Tune

Rain, rain, go a - way. Come a - gain some oth - er day.
Sun, sun, come on out. We all want to play and shout!

With accompaniment, student starts here:

🔊 46/47

Steady (♩ = 120)

61

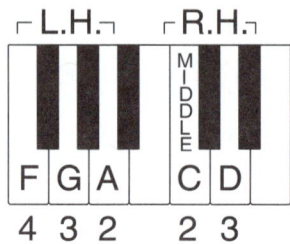

Dakota Melody

With a steady beat

R.H.

Native American

With accompaniment, student starts here: 🔊 **48/49**

With a steady beat (♩ = 120)

mf

pp

LOUD   or   *Soft?*

forte – f piano – p

Imagine the way each picture sounds.
Write p for soft or f for loud in the box below each picture.

Naming Notes on the Keyboard

Find the colored keys that match the colored boxes below.
To complete this story, write the letter names
of the keys in the colored boxes.

K__ti__ and M__rk s__t on th__ por__h,

playin__ musi__ __ames.

Soon th__ir da__'s voi__e spok__ to th__m __oth,

__allin__ out th__ir n__m__s.

"__rin__ me th__ pap__r i__ you will,"

he ☐sked ☐rom 'round the ☐oor.

Y☐t ☐oth o☐ the ☐hil☐ren, not wantin☐ to stop,

pl☐yed just ☐ minute mor☐.

When ☐in☐lly th☐y ☐inished and looke☐ for th☐ p☐per,

no si☐n o☐ it ☐ould they see,

Only ☐mpty ☐reen ☐rass with ☐resh mu☐☐y p☐w prints,

where ☐o you think it ☐ould ☐e?   Who took the paper?

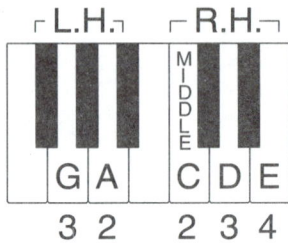

Quiet Night

Bill Boyd

Slowly

p

Snow - flakes ... gent - ly fall - ing. Sand - man ... sweet - ly call - ing.

Wind ... songs ... soft - ly stir - ring. Sleep with - out a ... care.

With accompaniment, student starts here: 🔊 **50/51**

Slowly (♩=88)

p

With pedal

66

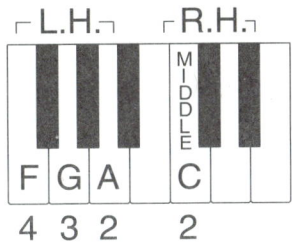

Knock-Knock Joke

L.H. F G A | R.H. MIDDLE C
4 3 2 | 2

With humor

R.H. **2**

Guatemalan

4/4 *f*

C

L.H. A
2

F
4

Knock on piano cabinet

G

× ×
"Knock - knock."

2

C

G
3

A
2

× ×
"Who's there?"

R.H. **2**

C

L.H. A
2

F
4

G

× ×
"Knock - knock."

2

C

G
3

F
4

× ×
"Who's there?"

With accompaniment, student starts here: 🔊 **52/53**

With humor
(♩ = 135)

mf

67

Knock-Knock Joke
(Activity Page)

🔊 52

As you listen to *Knock-Knock Joke*, follow the score in your lesson book and knock on the piano cabinet with your right hand every time you see:

Read & Discover

1. The music detective has come knocking at your door to ask you some questions about *Knock-Knock Joke*. Study the score and write your answers to the questions in the boxes below.

   Which finger always plays the R.H. quarter notes?

   What note does the R.H. play?

   Which L.H. finger do you skip in measure 1?

   Which finger plays G in measure 2?

2. Now the detective wants you to write the letter names of the missing notes in the boxes below. Add the finger numbers in the blanks below them.

With humor

R.H. **2**

C

4
4 *f*

L.H. **A**

2

F

4

"Knock - knock."

___

G

3

2

C

Guatemalan

"Who's there?"

___

R.H. **2**

C

L.H. **A**

2

F

4

"Knock - knock."

___

G

3

2

C

"Who's there?"

___

3. Tap your foot on ♩ ♩ as you play the song!

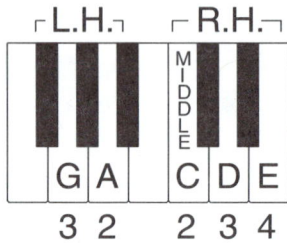

Old MacDonald Had A Band

With energy

R.H. 2

Old Mac-Don-ald had a band, E - I - E - I - O.
In his band he had a horn, E - I - E - I - O.

With accompaniment, student starts here: 🔊 54/55

With energy (♩ = 120)

70

R.H. **2**

Toot toot here. | Toot toot there. | Toot toot | ev - 'ry - where. |

L.H. **G** **3**

G **3**

R.H. **2**

Old Mac - Don - ald | had a band, | **4** E - I - E - I - O. |

L.H. **G** **A** **G** **3**

71

Rhythm Jam

When Old MacDonald's band began rehearsing music for its next show,
they discovered that some of the measures weren't complete.

Circle the one note or rest in the blue box
that will complete each measure.

Step or Repeat

The pig from Old MacDonald's Band is missing some of the note names from his favorite songs.

1. Using the arrows as guides, write the name of the mystery note in the blank above or below each one.
2. Play each two-measure example.

repeat	step up	step down
→	→	→

73

Playing Catch

Back and forth

With accompaniment, student starts here: 56/57

Back and forth (♩=110)

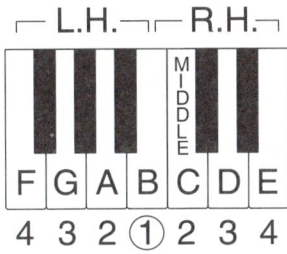

Popcorn

$\frac{4}{4}$

L.H. **A** 2   **F** 4   **G** 3   𝄾

f

R.H. **2** **C**   **4** **E**   **3** **D**   𝄾   **2** **C** ... **3** **G**   **2** **C** ... **3** **G**   **2** **C**   𝄾

With accompaniment, student starts here:

L.H.

🔊 **58/59**

Bouncy (♩=110)

$\begin{array}{}9:\\\end{array}$ $\frac{4}{4}$

mf

75

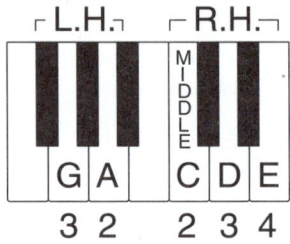

Bear Dance

Somewhat heavily

Christos Tsitsaros

With accompaniment, student starts here: 60/61

Somewhat heavily (♩ = 150)

76

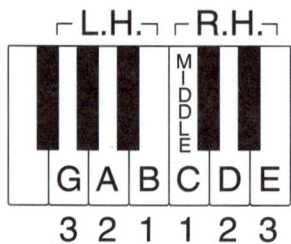

Stomp Dance

Carol Klose

Lively, with a steady beat

With accompaniment, student starts here: 🔊 62/63

Lively, with a steady beat (♩♪ = ♪♪) (♩ = 120)

AWARD CERTIFICATE

_____

HAS SUCCESSFULLY COMPLETED
HAL LEONARD ALL-IN-ONE
PIANO LESSONS, BOOK A
AND
IS HEREBY PROMOTED TO
BOOK B

_____   _____
TEACHER   DATE

HAL•LEONARD®

All-In-One Piano Lessons
Book A

GOLD AWARD MEDAL

HAL•LEONARD®

Cut-out may be fitted over student's shirt button.